GROWING UP

GROWING UP

Gospel Answers about
Maturation and Sex

BRAD WILCOX

BOOKCRAFT
SALT LAKE CITY, UTAH

Cover photo by Arthur Tilley/FPG International
Illustrations by Nathan Pinnock

Library of Congress Cataloging-in-Publication Data

Wilcox, Brad.
   Growing up : gospel answers about maturation and sex / Brad Wilcox.
     p.   cm.
   ISBN-10 1-57345-821-X (pbk.)
   ISBN-13 978-1-57345-821-4 (pbk.)
   1. Sex—Religious aspects—Mormon Church—Juvenile literature.   2. Sex—Religious aspects—Church of Jesus Christ of Latter-day Saints—Juvenile literature. [1. Sex—Religious aspects—Mormon Church.   2. Sexual ethics.]   I. Title.
   BX8643.S49 W55   2000
   241'.66'08822—dc21   00-037865

Printed in the United States of America
R. R. Donnelley

10 9   8   7

Dedicated to my former sixth-grade students—
it was a joy to be a part of your growing up

CONTENTS

CONTENTS

FOREWORD

A lot of books are available on human maturation and sex, but few of them address this sensitive topic in the context of Latter-day Saint beliefs, values, doctrines, and standards.

Many books describe sex as nothing more than a biological urge to be satisfied. Masturbation is considered okay—even healthy. Homosexuality is presented as an acceptable lifestyle. Teenagers are told that sex before marriage is all right as long as the partners really care about each other. Some books that attempt to offer values-based advice to young readers suggest only that those who engage in sexual activities be "safe" and "responsible." Such advice is wrong and is not compatible with our Heavenly Father's plan for our happiness.

This book focuses on the "facts of life" from an LDS perspective. Its author, Brad Wilcox, is uniquely qualified to do just that. Brad is an associate professor of education at Brigham Young University. Before that he taught sixth grade for three years (one of my sons was in his class). That's when he began teaching a boys' maturation clinic for his school district—something he continues to do in schools throughout Utah. This has given him front-line experience responding to questions that come from boys and their parents.

Brad also works with thousands of young people who attend Church Educational System youth programs, such as Especially for Youth. In addition, he serves as bishop of a student ward at Brigham Young University. Brad loves young people and is familiar with their needs, problems, pressures, and temptations.

As one who works with young people myself, I know how important it is that the issues in this book be addressed. As a medical doctor, I have reviewed the manuscript and found it to be accurate and informative.

Of course, parents have the primary responsibility for the sex education of their children. This book can be an aid to parents in that important endeavor. Sister Chieko N. Okazaki wrote, "For every child, there is something important about having someone outside the family explain a value held in the family. All parents need partners" (*Lighten Up!* [Salt Lake City: Deseret Book, 1993], 87). Perhaps through this book, Brad can be a partner with LDS parents in presenting the *right* information at the *right* time to help young people make the *right* choices as they grow up.

Thomas E. Myers, M.D.

ACKNOWLEDGMENTS

It is said that writers don't choose their topics, their topics choose them. That has certainly been the case with this book. The idea for this book has been "maturing" in my mind since I was asked to present my first "maturation clinic" in 1986. I wish to thank Lincoln Card, the principal at Edgemont Elementary School in Provo, Utah, where I taught sixth grade, for guiding me through my first years of teaching and for inviting me to teach the annual boys' maturation clinic.

I am grateful for my wife, Debi. As a registered nurse and a mother, she provided valuable insights and assistance in revising the manuscript. As my wife and best friend, she provided constant love and support upon which I have come to depend so heavily. I appreciate my parents, Ray T. and Val C. Wilcox, who reviewed the rough drafts of this book and responded with the same frankness I learned to expect from them when my brothers and I were growing up. I'm glad they were always willing to discuss sexual issues in an open, honest, and reverent way. I also appreciate my parents-in-law, Leroy and Mary Lois Gunnell, for their feedback and

ACKNOWLEDGMENTS

suggestions on the manuscript. And I thank Dr. Thomas E. Myers, who reviewed the book for accuracy and was willing to write the foreword. Thanks, Tom. You're the best.

My four children—Wendee, Russell, Whitney, and David—deserve prizes for the patience they have had with their dad. This time around Wendee and Russell deserve two extra gold stars. These teenagers provided valuable reactions and viewpoints. I'm thankful for their help, though I know it probably seemed weird to read a "sex book" written by their dad.

I must also acknowledge supportive friends: Hal and Barbara Jones, Kenneth and Kathy Cope, Clark and Julie Smith, and Ellen Allred. They helped me brainstorm and encouraged me to finish the project—especially when they saw what was and what wasn't available from other publishers on the same topic. I also wish to thank Emily Watts, Michael Morris, and the rest of the team at Deseret Book for being so wonderful to work with.

Finally, thanks to Brad Allen, a young priests quorum adviser who went many extra miles for me. I admire him and his family and will never forget his willingness to answer my questions and talk with me while I was growing up.

INTRODUCTION

A Word with Parents

It can feel awkward talking to children about maturation and sex, but it's important. If children do not initiate discussions, we must look for appropriate opportunities to bring up the subjects ourselves.

Some parents worry that by speaking frankly with their children about their bodies and sex, they are somehow promoting or condoning promiscuous behavior. My experience has taught me that the opposite is true. The most sexually active teens are usually the least informed. It is silence and ignorance, not open communication, that often leads to poor choices. The more solid sexual information young people gain from their parents, the more capable they are of making righteous and mature choices.

Regarding parental duty to teach children about sexuality, the First Presidency has said: "This responsibility cannot wisely be left to society, nor the schools: nor can the responsibility be shifted to the Church. It is the responsibility of parents to see that they fully perform their duty in this respect" (Conference Report, April 1969, 13).

Some awkwardness can be avoided if we talk to children about sex and maturation in private. Even family home evening may be too public a setting to be able to meet the needs of everyone gathered without embarrassing some and over-whelming others. Personal conversations allow us to teach more sensitively and effectively.

We need to be careful not to overload children with more information than they really need or want. I love the classic tale of the overanxious mother whose six-year-old asked, "Where did I come from?" When the mother launched into an oration on the facts of life, the little girl inter-rupted, "All I asked is where I came from. My friend Stephani says she came from Omaha."

The surest way to estimate just how much children know or want to know is to ask probing questions. For example, a child asks, "Where do babies come from?" A parent might reply, "What made you think of that?" Another child asks, "What does *adultery* mean?" The parent may respond, "What do *you* think it means?" A young teenage boy says, "I just don't understand girls?" A parent could ask, "Why? What do you mean?"

Probing questions are not an attempt to change the subject or avoid giving a straight answer. Rather, they offer a chance to listen as well as speak—to gather enough information so that we can respond effectively.

Once we have determined what a child knows and what we need to teach, we must not hesitate to say what needs to be said. We need to be factual, honest, and direct, even when we feel uneasy. It's okay to answer questions by saying, "I don't know everything, but I'll do my best" or "You know, I'm not quite sure about that. Let's find out together." Willingness to talk to our children, despite uneasiness, will strengthen our children's confidence in us.

While frankness is important in all the answers we provide, we should not resort to using gutter or slang terms in our discussions. Such terms communicate irreverence for a sacred topic. It may take a little effort on our part, but we can become comfortable calling body functions and parts by their proper names.

Sex doesn't have to be discussed grimly or solemnly. A light and positive touch can make discussion easier. Too often we unintentionally convey negative messages about our children's bodies and sexuality with our tone of voice and our words.

One father didn't exactly know how to respond when his sixth-grade son asked him about AIDS. The dad finally said gruffly, "AIDS has to do with sex, so you don't have to worry about it." The boy mustered his courage and said, "Well, what about sex?" The father fidgeted awkwardly and blurted, "Sex is the second worst sin next to murder."

Surely adultery and fornication are grave sins. However, this father unthinkingly conveyed a negative message about sex to his young son. If we are not careful, our children can get the idea that their bodies are ugly and that sex is dirty or bad. We must try to express ourselves in positive ways.

Fortunately, we are not alone. We can ask for help from Church leaders, relatives, doctors, family friends, teachers, or school counselors. A variety of reading materials is also available. This book has been written in an attempt to provide parents and young people with accurate information in the context of LDS values and standards. It is meant to be a resource for parents to use when young people ask questions about sex and growing up.

Children mature at different rates and will be ready to read, discuss, and ask questions about information in this book at different ages. When your children have questions about sex, you should do more than simply say, "Here, read this." Instead, you may want to read this book yourself first to become familiar with each chapter and with the italicized words that may be new to your children. Perhaps you will then be better prepared to discuss maturation issues with your children as you read the chapters together. It is hoped that you will find this book, written especially for young people between the ages of ten and fifteen, useful in opening doors of communication between you and your children.

A Shorter Word with Young People

As you read through this book, you are probably going to have questions. I hope you'll have the courage and maturity to ask someone who can provide the right answers. Talk to your parents, bishop, or another trusted adult. I know young people who think, *No way! I'm not talking about this stuff with my mom or dad!*

Instead, they talk to friends, cousins, or older brothers and sisters. It's true that kids closer to your age may be easier to talk to, but it's also true that they usually don't know what they are talking about. They pretend they do, and they want you to think they do, but don't settle for inaccurate information.

Your parents are the ones who have the knowledge, experience, and special interest in your eternal welfare to guide you along. You may feel awkward asking them personal questions, and they may feel awkward answering them. They may even squirm a bit or clear their throats a lot. That's okay. Just be patient. Your parents really do want to talk to you about this stuff. Believe it or not, they once went through exactly what you're going through and had most of the same questions you have. Give them a chance.

Chapter 1

CONCEPTION,
PRENATAL DEVELOPMENT,
AND BIRTH

In the Beginning

Some people say life begins at birth. Others say life begins when we first move inside our mothers. Still others claim life starts at *conception* when a man's sperm cell meets a woman's egg cell. They're all wrong. Life began long before any of these events.

We have a Heavenly Father and a Heavenly Mother who created our spirits before we came to earth. In that premortal existence we learned, grew, and progressed. Together with all our other spirit brothers and sisters, we wanted to become more like our heavenly parents. We all needed to come to earth, where we could obtain a physical body and have experiences that would allow us to learn, be tested, and reach our potential. Heavenly Father's plan gave each of us that opportunity.

Just as we have heavenly parents, we also now have earthly parents—a mother and a father who created bodies for our spirits.

≋

Smaller Than a Dot

When you began this physical life you were smaller than the period at the end of this sentence. In fact, that dot is way too big to describe how tiny the egg cell (or *ovum*) was that your mom provided. At the same time your mom provided that

9

egg cell, your dad provided a *sperm* cell that was even smaller. One egg cell is over ninety thousand times larger than a sperm cell.

While your mom provided one egg cell, your dad provided 200–500 million sperm cells. Despite their size difference, the egg cell and the sperm cell each contributed exactly one half of the *hereditary* material for your body.

⌢

You're the Winner

Of the millions of sperm cells that began the race to *fertilize* that egg cell, only about fifty actually reached it. The *reproductive* process is designed that way so that sperm cells with problems fall by the wayside. Of the fifty that reached the egg, only one actually penetrated and fertilized it. After fertilization, the outer wall of the egg changed remarkably and shut tight so other sperm cells could not enter. You could say that the fifty sperm cells that reached the egg were finalists, but only the very best won the race and made you. You started this physical life as a winner!

⌣

In Less Than a Day

Your dad's sperm cell and your mom's egg cell each carried half a blueprint or plan for your body. These blueprints are called *chromosomes*. These two blueprints formed a complete plan so

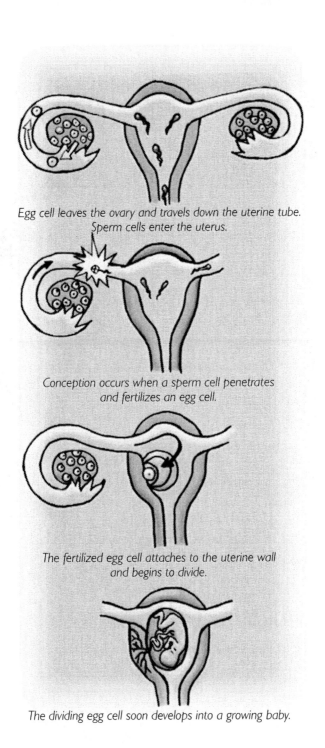

*Egg cell leaves the ovary and travels down the uterine tube.
Sperm cells enter the uterus.*

*Conception occurs when a sperm cell penetrates
and fertilizes an egg cell.*

*The fertilized egg cell attaches to the uterine wall
and begins to divide.*

The dividing egg cell soon develops into a growing baby.

that development of your mortal body could begin. Your *prenatal* development began when the fertilized egg cell started to divide. It only took about twelve hours for one cell to become two and another twelve hours for those two cells to become four. In less than a day your body was well under way.

⑥

Smile for the Camera!

If someone could have taken a picture of your body just two days after your dad's sperm cell and your mom's egg cell came together, you would be able to see the beginnings of your head, chest, and legs. Your mom probably wasn't even aware yet that she was *pregnant*, but there you were.

∧∧∧

Big Things in Little Packages

Inside your mom, you kept growing. After a month you were about the size one of your fingernails is now. Your brain and spinal cord were already forming, along with your lungs, stomach, and intestines. By one month, your heart, which started beating on about the eighteenth day, was now pumping strongly. Your arms and legs were even beginning to form.

〰〰

The Foot Bone's Connected to the Leg Bone ...

At about two months doctors stopped calling you an *embryo* (a Greek word meaning *to swell*) and began referring to you as a *fetus* (a Latin word meaning *young one*). Your bones had started to form, and by then your mom and dad knew you were coming. They called you their baby. At two months you were about the size the top half of your thumb is now. You had a face—eyes, ears, nose, and mouth—and all your major body systems were in place.

≋

Order Up!

All this growth was made possible because of the food you were receiving from your mom. You couldn't order and say, "I'll have pizza," but as your mom ate, her blood absorbed nutrients from the food. She then passed some of those nutrients to you as her blood flowed through the *umbilical cord* that connected you to her. The place where that cord once entered your body is your *navel* or belly button. It is through the umbilical cord that you also received oxygen because inside your mother you were sur-rounded by a salty fluid and could not breathe as you do now.

If a mother-to-be chooses to smoke, drink, or

take drugs, those destructive substances can be passed along to her baby through the umbilical cord. That's why it's so important for moms to avoid those harmful things.

@

Grow, Baby, Grow!

By three months you tripled and almost quadrupled the size you were at two months. Imagine what would happen if you kept growing at that same fast pace after you were born? By the time you were old enough to read this book, you would be so huge that no building could house you.

By three months, your teeth were forming, all your body systems were working, and you were beginning to look like you. A sonogram, which is a picture produced by ultrasound technology, could even reveal whether you were a boy or girl.

꒒

Move It!

At four months you were about the size your hand is now. Your mom could feel you moving inside her. It wasn't the first time you moved on your own, but it was the first time you were big enough for her to feel it. You also had fine hair beginning to grow.

꒔

Way to Flex

By the fifth month you were over six inches long. You were active and energetic, and you were busy flexing your developing muscles. By six months you could make a hard fist and seemed to delight in punching and kicking your mom, showing off your newfound strength. You had vocal cords and could have cried up a storm, except there was no air around you.

~

The BTC

You've heard of the MTC—Missionary Training Center. Well, we could call your last few months

inside your mom your BTC—Birth Training Center. It was a time for you to acquire additional strength, health, and immunity to disease. Babies can be born early and survive just as missionaries can go directly to their missions and perhaps survive without training. The MTC, though, sure makes the transition easier. It's the same with the BTC.

⑥

Happy Birthday!

After about nine months it was time for you to be born. Your birth was a painful and exhausting process for your mom, but she will be the first to tell you it was worth it.

Little children sometimes think that babies grow in moms' stomachs. Actually, you grew inside your mom's *uterus* or womb, which is below her stomach and is made of muscle. When it was time for you to be born, that muscle began to squeeze or contract and, after many hours of these labor pains, your mom's uterus finally pushed you out into her *vagina*, which stretched enough to let you come out between her legs.

If a birth is especially difficult, doctors may give the mother an operation called a *cesarean section,* during which they cut open her abdomen and uterus and lift the baby out. Doctors then stitch up where they cut the mother and she begins to heal.

Whether you came through your mother's vagina or were lifted out of her body during an operation, someone had to clamp off the umbilical cord and cut it. Because there are no nerves in the cord, it was a painless process. It took a week or two for the short stump of cord that was left on you to dry up and fall off, leaving only your belly button.

∧∧∧

Welcome to the World

I was with my wife for the births of our four children. I remember each birth in great detail. Some tense and nervous moments arose when things didn't go the way they should have. For long hours, I waited and watched Debi in labor. We were grateful for everyone who had helped us during each pregnancy, and we shed tears of joy when we held each baby for the first time. At those moments my wife and I enjoyed a feeling of closeness that was unforgettable.

Many in the world believe that your birthday is your beginning. How blessed we are to know that your birthday is really just your welcome-to-earth day. The first words I whispered to each of my children as I held them after their deliveries were, "Welcome to the world!"

∼∼
∼∼

Feeding Baby

Newborn babies are dependent on others. They can hardly do anything for themselves. They can't eat regular food or even baby food for awhile. One thing they can do is suck. Heavenly Father sends every newborn with an instinctive ability to suck milk from the *nipples* of its mother's breasts.

After a baby is born, the mother's body produces milk that has all the nutrients the baby needs to grow and be protected from disease. If for some reason a mother can't breast-feed her baby, the baby can be fed formula out of a bottle.

≋

What about Twins?

My wife has a twin brother. I'm always surprised at how many people ask her, "Are you identical?" A girl and a boy can't be identical twins! Debi and her brother are *fraternal* twins, which means they came from two different egg cells fertilized by two different sperm cells. They just shared the same growing space. My wife was born a few minutes before her brother. He likes to tell people he was being a gentleman by letting the lady go first.

Some twins are identical, meaning they look alike. They came from one egg cell that was fertilized by one sperm cell, but then the fertilized egg split and created two bodies. Even though

their bodies look alike, they are different people with different spirits.

Sometimes you hear about multiple births such as triplets, quadruplets, and quintuplets. Most of these multiple births are a combination of several possibilities—for example, one fertilized egg cell that splits into three babies, one set of identical twins, or two sets of twins. God has lots of ways of getting his spirit children to earth to receive their bodies.

@

Miscarriages and Abortions

Sometimes when a baby is developing inside its mother, something goes wrong. In that case, the baby dies and the mother's body lets the baby go early. It doesn't have the chance to be born and live like you did. The natural loss of a fetus during its development is called a *miscarriage*. Most often, babies are lost during the first three months of pregnancy. The loss of a developing baby is a sad time for parents.

An *abortion*, on the other hand, is not natural. An abortion occurs when someone ends a developing baby's life before it has the chance to be born and live like you. Most abortions are performed because the parents do not want the baby. Church members should not have, perform, encourage, or pay for abortions. Such actions have serious physical, emotional, and spiritual consequences. If a baby is unwanted, other options can be considered such as adoption.

Many people claim that a woman should have the right to abort her baby if she wants to. Not enough people are watching out for the rights of those babies who suffer innocently because of the bad choices of others. Church members follow the Lord's commandment: "Thou shalt not . . . kill, nor do anything like unto it" (D&C 59:6).

We Are Family!

We are all born into a family. Children who are adopted into their families can be sealed to them in the temple.

Today we live in a world where a lot of people are saying strange things about families. Some say that being a parent isn't very important and that children are a burden. Others say it is too

expensive to have children or that there are too many people on the earth.

These messages are wrong. Parenthood is the most important thing in the whole world. It's also very challenging. Children are a big responsibility. Taking care of them is difficult and expensive, but children are also a huge blessing and provide parents great joy that makes every sacrifice worthwhile. If we take care of the earth, it can support as many of Heavenly Father's spirit children as he sends.

Many of today's families are struggling. Parents are getting divorced, and family members of all ages are getting hurt. It is sad when these things happen—especially when some have to suffer because of the choices and actions of others. Since so many homes are in trouble, some say that the traditional family unit doesn't work and that we need to consider alternatives. That is not the case, so do not give up on family. The family unit is an eternal part of God's plan without substitute, alternative, or equal.

Chapter 2

KEYS TO EMOTIONAL, SOCIAL, INTELLECTUAL, AND SPIRITUAL GROWTH

I Put Money in the Change Machine, But I'm Still Me

Adolescence is a time of change. Changes that happen as we turn from children into adults can be a little scary, but don't be overly concerned. Every adult you know went through it, and every adult you admire went through it—your parents, your Church leaders, even the apostles and prophets. It is a normal and natural step in life. It is nothing to be afraid or ashamed of, just informed about. In the scriptures God has told us that those who are prepared have no need to fear (D&C 38:30).

Change is nothing new. In fact, it happens to us our whole lives. Whenever we grow, we grow emotionally, socially, intellectually, and spiritually. We grow physically too, but let's learn about the other areas first.

⌒

"Get Out of My Face!"

If you have teenage brothers or sisters, you have probably been told, "Get out of my face!" Your sister was just sitting there enjoying life and then suddenly she became angry, upset, or depressed. Such behavior is called a mood swing, and perhaps you've experienced one yourself. One minute you feel on top of the world, and the next minute you feel like the world is on top of you. Does anyone escape such extreme feelings during the teenage years? I'm afraid not, but that's not all bad. My wife, a nurse, says that when we are hooked to a heart monitor we don't want to see a straight line. It's the ups and downs that mean we're alive. In the same way, our highs and lows are evidence that we are living, learning, and growing emotionally.

∴

The Key to Emotional Growth: Responsibility

Each area of growth is like a locked door through which you must pass. A locked door is no problem if you have the key. The key to emotional growth is not to avoid or deny feelings but to take responsibility for them.

The second Article of Faith teaches that we will all be punished for our own sins. The word *own* means that our mistakes and sins belong to us and that we must admit that we alone are to blame for our poor choices. "It's the teacher's fault" or "My mom made me mad" or "He hit me first" just do not cut it as excuses. Situations may explain why we have strong feelings, but they do not excuse us from controlling our feelings.

If you have a horrible day, you allowed it to happen. If you have a wonderful day, you deserve the credit for staying positive. Other people do not have to change so you can feel better. You're the one who owns your life and must take responsibility for it.

⑥

"A Lot More World Out There"

The next locked door you face has to do with social growth. I like the story of the little boy who came running into the kitchen yelling, "Hey, Mom, you're never going to believe it!"

His mom stopped what she was doing and asked excitedly, "What am I not going to believe?"

"Well, I was in the backyard and I found a hole in the fence, and when I looked through, there was a lot more world out there."

Each passing year allows you to see more and more beyond your world's current boundaries. With more world come more people. This can be wonderful if you know how to handle yourself.

One teenage boy I will call Greg didn't handle himself very well. He said, "When I was in elementary school it was like I was in this cushioned environment. I had my best buddies and we formed clubs and built forts. Then I went to middle school with tons of other kids from all over the city. I didn't know anyone, and my friends all had different classes."

Greg felt alone, insecure, and out of place. What he didn't realize was that every kid in the school was going through a similar transition. Greg told me, "I knew I was cool, but it seemed like no one else did. How was I supposed to let everyone know I was cool without telling them I was cool, which is definitely not cool?"

Greg decided to try to make himself look better by making some other kids look stupid. He began teasing and making fun of his classmates. Greg said, "In P.E. I would find a wimpy kid who couldn't play sports as well as me and I'd start making a big deal of it. In my other classes I started making fun of anyone who looked different—like the kid with a big nose or frizzy hair. Everyone would laugh, so I just kept doing it."

Greg's plan wasn't very original—lots of other people had thought of it before. Nor did his plan work. Not only did the kids Greg picked on begin to avoid him, but everyone else started disliking Greg as well. Even those who were laughing on the outside were inwardly wondering when Greg would turn on them. Greg said, "I thought I was becoming so popular, but instead, the whole time, everyone was pulling away from me. I was actually losing the few friends I had."

∧᷿∧

The Key to Social Growth: Respect

The key to social growth is respect. As our world expands beyond the backyard fence, our social circles will also expand if we remember to respect others.

It doesn't matter if you are white and someone else is brown, black, green, purple, or striped. It doesn't matter if you are a Latter-day Saint and someone else belongs to another religion. It doesn't matter if you like volleyball and soccer and someone else likes singing, dancing, or playing the piano. It doesn't matter if you are young and someone else is old. We respect differences.

People like being around those who make them feel better. When you respect others, you help them feel important and included. They will like being with you, and your social world will grow.

Jesus taught a parable about a lost sheep. Remember the shepherd who left the "ninety and nine" to go in search of the one (Luke 15:4)? When I was younger I always felt bad for the ninety-nine who were left behind while the shepherd paid so much attention to just one. Now I realize that by caring so much about the one, the shepherd was also communicating his love for the ninety-nine. By seeking the lost sheep, the shepherd helped all the others feel more secure.

What if the shepherd had said, "Hey, I'm not going to take time to go find that dumb lost sheep. He has a big nose and frizzy wool anyway." Even if the ninety-nine laughed, they probably would have been thinking, *Is that how he is going to act when I get lost?* Gossiping about one sheep behind its back sends a clear message to ninety-nine others that you are capable of doing the same thing to them one day. The key to social growth is showing respect—to people's faces *and* behind their backs.

～～

Get a Brain

What's the difference between the Scarecrow in the *Wizard of Oz* and a couch potato? The Scarecrow *knew* he didn't have a brain. Intellectual growth is learning to love learning. Watch how little kids discover pure pleasure in the process of poking, prying, and playing. Don't allow yourself to lose that ability.

One day when I was teaching sixth grade I began class by announcing, "Today is the anniversary of the gunfight at the OK Corral."

"What?" one of the students asked. I could tell that I had sparked some interest.

"You've never heard of the OK Corral?" I asked.

"No. Tell us about it," responded another student.

"I'm not going to tell you about it," I said. "But there's a book in the library that will tell you all about it."

I then went to warn the librarian that she

would soon be stormed by my entire class searching for the same book. At the end of the day when I asked the librarian how many students had come searching for the book, she replied, "One."

Only one out of my whole class! I was disappointed. At the very time when these young students should have been taking off intellectually, they were apathetically allowing themselves to ignore great opportunities.

≈

The Key to Intellectual Growth: Reading

The key to intellectual growth is reading. It's time to turn off the TV, the Nintendo, and the computer games long enough to turn on to some good books!

Everyone says there is too much sex, too much violence, and too much negative behavior on TV. But I'll tell you one more too much: too much TV. Most kids watch around twenty-four hours of TV every week. That means they spend almost one full day per week in front of the television. If you're like most kids, by the time you're eighteen you will have spent more time watching TV than doing any other single activity except sleeping.

Grandparents are fond of saying, "If something is worth doing, it's worth doing well." Let's

switch it around and say that if something is *not* worth doing, it's not worth doing well. Think of how many books you could finish by trading even a fraction of your TV time for some good reading.

Have you ever read a book and then seen a movie made from the book? Were you disappointed? Most people are. That's because reading is a mentally active experience while watching TV is a mentally passive one. When we watch TV or a video, we do not have to imagine the setting. It is shown to us. We do not have to imagine what the main characters look like. They are shown to us. We do not even have to imagine the kissing scenes because—like it or not—those are shown to us too. On the other hand, reading allows us to use our brains and grow intellectually.

I compliment you for reading this book. You are following Paul's counsel to "give attendance to reading" in your youth (1 Timothy 4:13). Keep up the great work. Keep reading magazines, newspapers, cereal boxes, bumper stickers—anything you can get your eyes on. Keep reading good books—famous ones, fun ones, sad ones, spiritual ones. Keep reading and you will come to understand why the comedian Groucho Marx once said, "Outside of a dog, man's best friend is a book; inside of a dog, it's too dark to read."

@

Goliath Was a Spiritual Shrimp

Another way we grow is spiritually. Too often we neglect our spiritual growth. What is spiritual growth? One little child said, "It's when your inside gets bigger than your outside."

In the Old Testament we read about how much bigger Goliath was than David. Spiritually, however, young David was a giant compared to his opponent. A similar comparison could be made among the sons of Lehi in the Book of Mormon. Laman and Lemuel may have been older, perhaps even bigger, but Nephi and Sam were light-years ahead of their brothers spiritually.

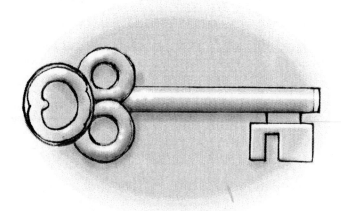

Area of Growth	Key
Emotional	Taking **Responsibility** for our emotions
Social	**Respecting** others
Intellectual	**Reading** good books
Spiritual	**Remembering** the Savior, our covenants, and who we really are

The Key to Spiritual Growth: Remember

The key to the door of spiritual growth is one word: remember. We must remember the Savior, our covenants, and who we really are. We must remember the sacrifices of the many people who came before us and who enabled us to enjoy the freedoms and advantages we have today. As we remember all these things, we will feel more motivated to pray, read scriptures, and seek the positive environments that will foster spiritual growth.

The prophet Alma gave his son Helaman some wise counsel when he said, "Let all thy thoughts be directed unto the Lord; yea, let the affections of thy heart be placed upon the Lord forever. Counsel with the Lord in all thy doings, and he will direct thee for good" (Alma 37:36–37). We know our spirits are growing when we fill our minds with thoughts of the Savior, our hearts with love of the Savior, and our lives with acts of the Savior (Robert E. Wells, *We Are Christians Because . . .* [Salt Lake City: Deseret Book, 1985], 108).

Chapter 3

PHYSICAL GROWTH

"Am I Normal?"

Physical growth is the most obvious way in which we change as we grow up. If there were a key word related to physical growth, it would be *relax!* Calm down! Don't be overly concerned!

Physical maturation is controlled by the *pituitary gland,* which is located inside your head just under your brain. When the time is right for you, the pituitary gland sends a signal to your body to begin changing you from a child into an adult.

For some, this change begins when they are around ten, eleven, or twelve. For others, it begins between thirteen and sixteen. For a few, it begins very naturally when they are seventeen or eighteen. Girls usually mature earlier than boys.

Perhaps the biggest question on the minds of young teenagers is, "Am I normal? Are the changes that are or are not happening to me normal?" With few exceptions, the answer is yes! If you begin changing before or after your friends, don't worry. Your body knows what is best for you and will take care of itself. Just relax.

〰

Growing a Foot or Two

Remember the Primary song about being a missionary when you have grown a foot or two? Well, one of the first physical changes you will notice is that you will get taller. You may even shoot up quite a bit in a relatively short time.

When I taught sixth grade, one boy would go out to the monkey bars at recess and dangle by his arms. After a while I approached him and said, "Wow, you're going to have the strongest arms in school!"

"Mr. Wilcox, I don't care if I'm strong," he replied. "I just want to be tall."

I had to explain that as much as he would like to, there was no way he could stretch himself. How tall you are going to be is pretty well determined by who your parents and grandparents are. You have to trust your body to know what is right for you.

⁛

Hungry Again?

"How can you be hungry again?" your mom asks. "We just ate."

Because your body is growing, you need more food to give you energy. That's okay. Just make sure you are filling up on the healthy foods your parents and teachers talk about. Avoid the junk food that may satisfy your hunger but will not help you grow the way you want to.

During teenage years most young people become aware of their weight. Many feel they are "too fat," though some feel they are "too thin." A nutritious diet and regular exercise can help, but everyone has a basic body type that does not change no matter how much dieting and exercise they do. Some people have rounder, stockier bodies with more body fat. Others are more muscular with wide shoulders and slim hips. Still others are slim with sharp features and very little body fat.

People with bigger builds may look heavier than their smaller-built friends, even if they weigh exactly the same. It's easy to become discouraged if you spend too much time comparing yourself to professional athletes, movie stars, and super models. Chances are you don't look much like they do.

You have to remember that many of the "perfect" bodies that bombard you daily have been manufactured and manipulated through make-up, plastic surgery, steroids, or enhanced photography to appear better than they really are. You also have to keep in mind that everyone has something he or she would like to change—even the super models. While you wish to be thinner, someone who is thinner wishes for your hair. While you wish to be stronger, someone who is stronger wishes for your complexion.

Weight and looks are a temporary and shaky foundation on which to build self-worth. Feelings of self-worth must be grounded in the knowledge that we are God's children and that he has a plan for our lives. As we focus on who we are and on our eternal potential for development, we can keep a positive outlook.

@

Bigfoot

When you consider how your feet, hands, arms, and legs are growing to keep up with the trunk of your body, you may think the legend of Bigfoot is no legend at all. Different parts of the body grow at different times. Among the earliest parts of the body to reach full size are hands and feet, so for awhile they may seem large in proportion to the rest of your body. This growth can cause you to feel awkward at times. You may feel as if you can't quite run, jump, dance, or even walk like you used to.

You will knock over a few milk cartons and skin some knees as you try to get everything moving in the same direction. Just be patient with yourself (and remind your parents to be patient with you too). You'll get accustomed to your new and improved body soon enough.

∿∿

Zits Are the Pits

As you grow you'll notice that your skin becomes more oily. If your skin did not have oil, or *sebum*, it would become so hard and dry you could not move. When you are a teenager your oil glands are more active than ever—especially those on your face, back, shoulders, and chest. That's okay except when the oil gets backed up in the ducts of the enlarged oil glands. When that happens, you can develop *pimples* or zits.

Zits do not come from eating too much chocolate or greasy food, though diet can affect your complexion. They do not even come from dirty skin, but dirt can contribute to the problem. They come from what is happening underneath the surface of your skin. The best thing you can do is wash your face regularly and try to keep your hands away from your face. But you could wash your face a hundred times a day and still have skin problems. If your skin gets too bad, your parents can get you the medicine you need.

~~~

Soap (and Other New Words)

Along with being oily, you will also sweat more. Sweat is one way your body keeps cool and, believe it or not, sweat does not smell. The smell actually comes from bacteria that grow in warm, dark, moist places. Where is it warmer, darker, and moister than under your arms or inside your shoes after a good game of soccer?

The best way to avoid odor is by cleaning away the bacteria. Take a bath or shower regularly, and when you are in the shower, don't just stand there and watch the water run. Use soap (I hope that's not a new word in your vocabulary), and clean yourself in those warm, dark, moist places. Also, wash your hands after using the bathroom, change your underwear every day, and brush your teeth regularly.

~~~

Hair Where?

Hair offers our bodies some protection and insulation as well as giving us a pleasing appearance. As you grow older you will notice the hair that already grows on your arms and legs will become a bit darker, coarser, and thicker. You will also start seeing hair grow on parts of your body where hair hasn't grown before: Under your arms and between your legs, for example.

Hair growing between your legs in the *pubic* area is one of the best indicators that your pituitary gland has sent the signal and that you are growing up physically and have reached *puberty*. In fact, the word puberty comes from the Latin word *pubertas,* which means "to become covered as with hair." Pubic hair may be the same color as the hair on your head, or it may be lighter or darker. It's usually curlier than the hair on your head.

Some boys will grow hair on their chests and faces as well. Most boys shave their facial hair, and most girls shave their legs and under their arms.

@

A Wonderful Gift

Some religious groups see our physical bodies as a burden, a problem, a temporary hindrance from which we will one day be free. They see the body as ugly, sinful, or bad. Latter-day Saints know that is not true. Joseph Smith said, "We came to this earth that we might have a body and present it pure before God in the celestial kingdom. The great principle of happiness consists in having a body. The devil has no body, and herein is his punishment" (*Teachings of the Prophet Joseph Smith* [Salt Lake City: Deseret Book, 1976], 181).

God the Father and Jesus Christ possess perfected, glorified, tangible, resurrected bodies. Our bodies were created in God's image. Some of the greatest tests, challenges, and lessons of our lives are associated with our bodies, which have appetites and needs that are new to our spirits.

These bodies serve as temples for our spirits during mortality and will be ours forever in the Resurrection. What a wonderful gift! We have something Satan and his followers will never have. No wonder it is so important to take care of our bodies.

Caring for our bodies is a sacred stewardship and duty. We are commanded to avoid tobacco, alcohol, and drugs. At the same time, we must give our bodies the food, rest, physical exercise, and recreation they need. That's why the Church "was the first religious organization to construct halls adjacent to or adjoining chapels for the formal promotion of . . . games and sports, music, drama, speech, and dance" (in Daniel H. Ludlow, ed., *Encyclopedia of Mormonism,* 5 vols. [New York: Macmillan Publishing, 1992], 3:1081).

By practicing good *hygiene*, living the Word of Wisdom, and being physically active, we show respect for ourselves and we show appreciation to God for giving us each such a wonderful gift.

·*(-·*

Modesty

Another way we can thank Heavenly Father for the gift of our bodies is by being modest and avoiding tight-fitting or revealing clothes and extremes in dress and appearance. The body is beautiful, but there are certain parts of the body that should be special and private.

In *For the Strength of Youth,* the First Presidency teaches that wearing immodest bathing suits and clothing sends a strong message that you are using your body to get attention and approval. Such attention and approval is short-lived and not the kind that builds true self-worth or prepares you for a strong and healthy marriage. We should dress so that the first thing others notice about us is our face.

Chapter 4

ABOUT BOYS

The Basics

A boy has a *penis* and two *testicles* between his legs. The testicles hang underneath the penis in a sack of skin called the *scrotum*. One testicle usually hangs a little lower than the other to keep them from bumping into each other when a boy walks.

At the end of the penis is a small opening where *urine* (and eventually sperm cells) comes out. The sperm cells allow the boy to one day become a father.

The boy's sex organs or *genitals* are outside his body because the sperm cells have to be made and stored at a slightly cooler temperature than the boy's normal body temperature. The scrotum acts as a temperature-control gauge. When it's cold outside, the scrotum constricts, pulling the testicles closer to the body so they can be warm. When it's warm outside, the scrotum relaxes so the testicles can hang lower and stay cool.

As a teenage boy becomes a man, his testicles and scrotum become larger and a bit darker in color. His penis will also get longer and wider than it was when he was a child. The penis and testicles are very sensitive. When a boy is engaged in strenuous physical activity, he should wear an athletic supporter or dance belt—something that offers support and protection.

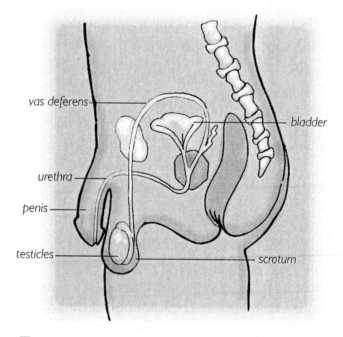

Testosterone

When it is time for a boy to change into a man, the pituitary gland sends a signal to the testicles. Then, along with producing sperm cells, the testicles also start producing testosterone, which is the male *hormone* that flows through the boy's body and is responsible for initiating the changes he will experience during puberty.

∴

Broadened Shoulders, Barreled Chest

When a boy's arms and legs are growing, his shoulders begin to broaden and his chest begins to barrel out. It is also natural for a boy's breasts to swell a bit and his nipples to stick out. The *areola* or colored circle of skin around the nipple will get darker and wider. When that happens a boy may panic and think, *Oh great! I'm turning into a girl!*

No need to worry. Some breast swelling is normal for a boy, who may also notice hard, rocklike bumps forming inside his nipples. These can be tender and sore. That's okay. It is just one of the ways the body adjusts to its new hormones. It can take up to a year and a half for this condition and discomfort to pass, but it will usually pass. The swelling stops and, as a boy's chest expands, this condition becomes less noticeable.

⑥

Voice Changes

Many boys experience the embarrassment of answering the phone and having the caller assume they are their sister. A boy may think, *What's the matter? Can't they see I'm a boy?* No, not on the phone. They can only hear you. A young boy's vocal cords are similar to a girl's vocal cords: thin and short.

Think of a piano. The thin, short strings produce high sounds. The long, thick strings produce the low sounds. As boys grow their vocal cords become longer and thicker and their voices deepen. Their voice boxes will sometimes stick out. That's okay. One side of a grand piano sticks out farther than the other side. The male hormones cause changes in the angle of the Adam's apple, and that part of a boy's throat may become more noticeable.

When these changes start happening some boys' voices will crack or suddenly shift from a lower to a higher pitch. They may feel embarrassed when their voices sound high or squeaky, but they do not need to. A cracking voice just means they're growing up.

∧∧∧

Circumcision

Every boy is born with a fold of skin called the *foreskin* that covers the end of his penis. Some parents choose to have a small operation performed on their sons to remove it. The operation is called *circumcision*. Boys who were circumcised do not remember it because it happened when they were babies. A boy who has not been circumcised still has a piece of skin around the top of his penis. If a boy wonders whether he was circumcised, he can always ask his mom or dad.

For boys who are not circumcised, the word to remember is cleanliness. When an uncircumcised boy is in the shower, he should pull the fold of skin back and clean the end of his penis completely with soap. For all boys, the word to remember along with cleanliness is respect. If a circumcised boy is in a public shower or locker room and happens to see a boy who has not been circumcised, he should not tease, point, or stare. The uncircumcised boy should not tease, point, or stare either. We respect other people, regardless of differences.

〜〜

Nocturnal Emissions

Sperm cells made in the testicles are stored in coiled tubes attached to the top and rear of each testicle called the *epididymis.* The epididymis is like a boy's personal water balloon. It fills with sperm cells until they are mature. Then one night when the boy is asleep his body releases those sperm cells. They travel up narrow tubes called the *vas deferens* and combine with fluids. This mixture is called *semen* and exits the boy's body through his penis. This involuntary *ejaculation* is called a *nocturnal* (occurring at night) *emission.*

Semen and urine both leave the body through the penis. That's why when most boys have their first nocturnal emission, they may think they wet the bed. But urine and semen are different fluids. Urine is a body waste. It is stored in the bladder and has nothing to do with the reproductive system. Urine is thin, watery, yellowish, and produced by the cupful. Semen is creamier in color, thicker in texture, and produced by the tea-spoonful. Urine and semen cannot come out of the penis at the same time. A special valve at the base of the bladder closes off the urine during ejaculation of semen.

Nocturnal emissions are sometimes called wet dreams—"wet" because the boy's bed or under-wear may be slightly wet from the semen that has been ejaculated, and "dream" because it hap-pens during sleep. Some boys wake up. Others do not notice anything has happened until morn-ing. Either way, wet dreams are a normal part of growing up and becoming a man. They are noth-ing to be ashamed of. When they happen a boy should think, *Good! I'm normal. My body works.* Then he should change his underwear and sheets. If his mom wonders why he is changing his sheets, the boy can simply say, "Last night I had a wet dream." Parents know what you are talking about, but it's not something to announce at the breakfast table or at school. It's a private thing between you and your parents.

It is hard to say how often wet dreams will occur. For some boys they will happen weekly. For others, depending on different circum-stances, they will happen once every six months or once a year. A boy must trust his body to know what is best for him.

Some boys feel bad because they remember having a "sexy" dream during their nocturnal emission. But they can no more control their dreams than they can control the constriction of their pupils when someone shines a flashlight in their eyes. Thus, they cannot be held accountable for dreams and should not feel bad about them. It's okay to leave such dreams behind and begin the day in peace. Remember, however, that we are responsible for our thoughts while we're awake.

≈

Erections

Now and then spongy tissue inside a boy's penis will fill up with blood. When this happens his penis becomes long and hard and sticks out from his body at an angle. It may even curve slightly. Boys usually hear a lot of slang words describing this normal reaction, but the actual term is *erection*. There is no bone in the penis even though it can get so stiff it feels like a bone. Some erections happen slowly and others very quickly. Some last awhile; others disappear quickly. It all depends on the boy and the situation.

Because this doesn't usually happen in front of other people, a boy sometimes feels that it happens only to him. Nothing could be further from the truth. It happens to every boy and every man regularly. Sometimes an erection is associated with *sexual* thoughts, but sometimes it is associated with other strong emotions like nervousness, fear, or excitement. It may even happen when a boy's bladder is full and he needs to go to the bathroom. Erections sometimes happen for no particular reason at all. When they happen, the best thing for a boy to do is think, *Good! I'm normal. My body works.* Then he can focus on something else and let his body take care of itself.

Sometimes a boy might worry that his penis is too small. When penises are soft they vary in length and size. However, no matter how long or short a penis is when it is relaxed, the erections of adult men are approximately the same size (six to seven inches). Understand that the size of a man's penis doesn't affect how it functions.

@

How Embarrassing!

It's normal to feel a little embarrassed when people talk about the functions of our bodies. However, it's important to remember that our bodies are not dirty or nasty, evil or bad. They are God-given. Private does not necessarily mean secret or sinful.

Chapter 5

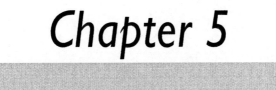

ABOUT GIRLS

The Basics

A girl has a *vagina*, a *uterus*, and two *ovaries*. These reproductive organs are inside her abdomen, where they are warm and protected. The ovaries store the egg cells or ova that can allow the girl to one day become a mother. Unlike boys, who don't start producing sperm cells until puberty, girls are born with all their eggs (about 250,000), which start maturing at puberty. The ovaries sit on either side of the uterus or womb and are connected to it by two tubes called *uterine* tubes (sometimes called *fallopian* tubes). The uterus is where a baby grows and develops before it is born. The vagina is a muscular tube that forms a passageway from the uterus to outside the girl's body between her legs. This area is called the *vulva*.

At the front of the vulva is a small opening, where urine comes out. Just behind this opening is the entrance to the vagina. Along the sides of the vulva are folds of skin called the inner and outer *labia*. Between the labia is a sensitive area called the *clitoris*.

As a teenage girl becomes a woman, her sex organs or genitals get larger and change position. Before puberty the uterus is straight up and down in a girl's body next to her bladder. During puberty, the back side of the vagina grows more than the front. This tilts the uterus forward over the bladder. Since these changes are happening inside a girl's body, she may not be aware of them.

A woman's uterus is about the size of a clenched fist, and it is very elastic. It has to be stretchable so a baby can grow inside it.

ॐ

Estrogen

A young girl's body changes when her pituitary gland sends a signal to her ovaries. Along with storing egg cells, the ovaries begin producing *estrogen*, the female hormone that flows through the girl's body and is responsible for initiating the changes she will experience during puberty.

⌢

Breasts

When a girl approaches womanhood, the areas around her nipples grow into breasts that can make milk for a baby. First, the nipple and the *areola* or colored circle of skin around the nipple get larger and darker. Then a small, flat, buttonlike bump develops in each nipple. As time goes on, the breasts usually become larger and fuller.

Most girls find their breasts feel tender, sore, or even downright painful when they are developing. This will pass in time. Girls may also discover that each breast may not develop at the same time; one may grow a bit faster than the other. There is no need to worry. The other one will catch up in a short time. Even so, most mature women have one breast that is a little larger than the other. This is normal.

Breasts are made up of fatty tissue and milk glands. They come in a variety of shapes and sizes. Some girls are concerned that their breasts are too small or too large, but when it comes to producing and storing milk for a baby, size doesn't matter at all. Exercise can make the chest muscles thicker, making breasts appear a bit larger, but the actual size of the breasts cannot be increased through exercise.

Most girls wear bras, though it is not absolutely necessary. Bras help girls to be modest, and most women feel more comfortable and confident with the support of a bra. A bra can also sometimes help to relieve the tenderness a girl feels as her breasts develop.

Body Shape

When a girl goes through puberty, her breasts are not the only things that become larger. Her hips widen, which can make her waist appear smaller. Overall, her body becomes more curvy and rounded.

Menstrual Periods

Remember that babies are fed with the blood that flows through the umbilical cord. When an egg cell leaves the ovary and begins traveling down the uterine tube, the lining of the uterus prepares to feed a baby by filling with blood. If the egg cell doesn't find a sperm cell, the egg cell and the blood-rich lining of the uterus simply wash out of the girl's body through her vagina. The next month the egg cell leaves the other ovary and the process repeats itself. This process happens over and over (except while a woman is pregnant) until she is well into her forties. Because this process happens periodically, or regularly, it is often referred to as a *period*.

Girls begin having periods or *menstruating* at different ages—some as early as ten and others at sixteen or seventeen. Once they have begun, periods usually happen about every month and last around three to seven days. However, the regularity and length of periods may vary—especially during teenage years.

Menstruating is different from urinating. Urine comes through the urinary opening. It is thin, watery, and yellowish. *Menstrual* fluid comes through the vagina. It is thicker and darker than urine because it is made up of blood and the velvety tissue that lines the uterus. It can sometimes look bright red, pink, or brown. A girl has control over when she urinates but has no control over when she menstruates. Urination takes little time. Menstruation, however, takes longer because the menstrual fluid drips out slowly. A girl may shed as little as a tablespoon of menstrual fluid during her period or as much as a cup. Sometimes—especially upon waking in the morning—a girl may notice thick clumps of blood or clots in her menstrual fluid. That also is normal.

Some girls tend to lose blood most heavily on the first few days of their periods and then trickle off. Others bleed lightly at first and then get heavier. Still others bleed for a few days, stop for a day, then start again. All of these patterns are considered normal. In fact, it is even normal to have different patterns from period to period. Girls just have to trust their bodies to know what is best for them.

∧∿∧

Menstrual Hygiene

Menstruation does not need to stop a girl from showering, swimming, running, or participating in any activity she wishes. She just needs to protect herself from embarrassment. At a drugstore or supermarket parents can help their daughters buy sanitary napkins or pads that can be worn inside their underwear to absorb the menstrual flow. The pads come with adhesive on one side so they stay in place. A girl wearing a pad may feel self-conscious—especially the first few times. However, no one else can tell when she is wearing a pad.

Another type of feminine protection is a tampon. Tampons are small plugs of absorbent material that can be inserted into the vagina. If they are inserted properly they cannot be felt and can't fall out. No one can tell when they are being used, and they don't interfere with regular urination or bowel movements. Tampons are removed by pulling on a short string that is left hanging outside the vagina. Because of a disease called toxic shock syndrome, it is best not to wear a tampon all the time. Some girls will alternate between tampons and pads during the day. Tampons should not be worn at night.

Pads and tampons should be changed every three or four hours or even more often when the menstrual flow is heavy. Menstrual blood itself does not smell, but when it leaves the uterus and comes in contact with germs, the germs grow rapidly and can cause an unpleasant odor. Girls can avoid problems by frequently changing pads and tampons, and by bathing or showering daily.

Used pads should be wrapped in toilet paper and placed in the trash or in a container for used sanitary napkins. Do not try to flush them down the toilet because they can clog the plumbing. Tampons, on the other hand, may be flushed down the toilet after they are used. A girl needs to always remember to wash her hands before and after changing pads or tampons.

Since girls may not know exactly when their periods are going to begin, they should keep a pad or tampon handy in a purse or locker. If a girl gets menstrual fluid on her underwear or clothes, she needs to soak them in cold water (hot water makes the stain worse), and then wash them normally.

Taking care of themselves during their periods can be a hassle for girls, but so can styling hair or caring for fingernails. Menstruation is just something girls need to learn how to manage as they grow up. When her first period arrives, a girl should think, *Good! My body works.* She may want to tell her mom or dad, but there's no need to broadcast it to the world. It is a private and personal thing.

Cramps

Some girls get mild to moderate cramps in their abdomens when they menstruate or during the week before. Cramps are perfectly normal and do not usually last long, but they can be uncomfortable.

Exercise may help. A girl can lie flat on the floor as if she were going to do a push-up. Then she can push her head and shoulders off the floor and arch her back without lifting her abdomen. Another exercise a girl can try begins with her lying on her side. She then brings her knees to her chest, points her chin down, and tries to touch her chin to her knees. Another exercise that seems to help is for the girl to lie flat on the floor, face down. Then she bends her knees and lifts her feet. Next, she stretches her arms behind her and grabs her ankles. As she gently rocks back and forth she may find some relief from cramps.

Medication may also help, but if cramps become severe or persist after a period ends, a girl should check with her doctor. Extremely painful periods can be treated.

PMS

Premenstrual syndrome or PMS is a medical condition that can produce a variety of physical and psychological symptoms. The symptoms usually show up a week or two before menstruation and end once a girl's period ends.

Physical symptoms may include bloating, weight gain, breast pain, backaches, headaches, and a craving for sweets. Psychological symptoms may include tension, depression, absent-mindedness, irritability, and sleep problems.

The causes of PMS are not well known, but it is believed that nutrition, body chemistry, and hormones all play a part. Some girls find they can relieve symptoms by eating high-protein foods, limiting salt intake, and avoiding caffeine. Regular exercise may also help.

If problems are severe, check with a doctor. Perhaps one of the best things a girl can do is be patient with herself and understand that there really are some normal things happening inside her over which she has little control.

@

It's a Miracle

Whenever we talk about how our bodies function, it is easy to lose perspective. Some people say menstruation is "disgusting" and even refer to it as "the curse." Actually, the body with all its complexities is one of the greatest evidences of

God's creative hand and incredible power. The body with all its functions truly is a marvelous gift from God.

Chapter 6

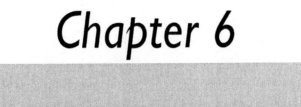

LOVE, MARRIAGE, AND SEX

What Is Love?

If you look for examples of love in the movie theater, on TV, or in teen magazines, you will probably find a lot of confusion. That's because many people confuse sex with love. If you look for examples of love in the scriptures, you will find the truth:

"Charity suffereth long, and is kind, and envieth not, and is not puffed up, seeketh not her own, is not easily provoked, thinketh no evil, and rejoiceth not in iniquity but rejoiceth in the truth, beareth all things, believeth all things, hopeth all things, endureth all things. . . . Charity is the pure love of Christ, and it endureth forever" (Moroni 7:45–47).

Romantic attraction and expression is an important part of love between a husband and a wife, but it is only a part. Sex and love generate different emotions, and husbands and wives learn to combine them.

·↲·

Crushes

Most little boys do not usually like most little girls and vice versa. But at about age ten or eleven, one particular boy or girl suddenly seems captivating. The strong attraction for another person is called a crush.

I remember my first crush. I had it when I was ten. The girl was in my class at school and also

in my ward. Our schoolteacher brought a camera to school and named me the class photographer. I was to take pictures of classmates throughout the year. I finished a whole roll of film the first day. When the teacher had the film developed and found that every picture was of one particular girl, he asked someone else to be the photographer from then on.

You can have a crush on someone you know or on someone you have only seen across the room or on the movie screen. It could be someone your own age or someone older like a teacher or your friend's older brother or sister. Crushes are the first romantic feelings young people have. They are normal, and everyone has them at one time or another. They usually last only a few days or weeks, and then you become interested in someone else.

⌢

Dating and Courtship

A date occurs when a young man and a young woman get together for an activity. It could be formal like going out for dinner and a dance or informal like going on a hike or picnic. As Latter-day Saints, we don't date before age sixteen and avoid pairing up and dating just one person until after high school and missions. We also date only those who share our same high standards. Many teenagers find the best and most comfortable dates occur when groups of friends get together and do something creative and fun.

After a young man returns from a mission, he looks for a young lady who shares many of his interests and goals. When he finds her, he begins to spend a lot of time with her. As their friendship deepens over time, the two lose interest in being with others. Ultimately they become engaged to be married. This process is called courtship.

∵

Marriage

Marriage occurs when a man and a woman become legally man and wife. They join their lives in every way. Latter-day Saints realize that

marriage is not just a cultural expectation or a nice tradition. Marriage is vital to the exaltation of every person. Deciding who to marry is one of the most important decisions of your life, but equally important is deciding where you will marry. President Howard W. Hunter said, "Let us reaffirm more vigorously than we ever have in the past that it does matter where you marry and by what authority you are pronounced man and wife" ("Follow the Son of God," *Ensign*, November 1994, 88). The place needs to be the temple, and the authority needs to be the priesthood sealing power found there.

I once read a newspaper story in which a reporter shared humorous responses from kindergarten children who were asked to define some difficult words. One of the words was *marriage.* The reporter liked the definition one child offered: "That's when you get sealed." The reporter spent the rest of the article reflecting on what an insightful and wonderful definition of marriage that was—to be bonded, linked, made secure. Little did he know that he had probably stumbled upon a young Latter-day Saint.

When couples are sealed in the temple they kneel across an altar from each other and look into mirrors on opposite walls that reflect their images endlessly. The mirrors symbolize the eternal nature of marriage. The Lord has said, "Whatsoever you seal on earth shall be sealed in heaven; and whatsoever you bind on earth, in my name and by my word, saith the Lord, it shall be eternally bound in the heavens" (D&C 132:46).

@

Sex

Sometimes people use the word *sex* to describe what you are—either male or female. But usually the word is used to describe certain acts, feelings, and experiences.

After a man and a woman marry, they have God's permission to have children. The process of creating children, or *procreation*, brings the husband and wife closer together than they ever could be in any other way. As an expression of their unity, feelings, commitment, and love, they talk, hold hands, hug, and kiss just as they did before they were married. But they also lie down together and stroke and touch each other in sexual places. These special expressions of affection are sacred and should never be shared outside of marriage.

A husband's body and a wife's body are made so they fit together. Just as a married man and woman are to be one spiritually, their bodies are made so that they can be one physically through the process of *sexual intercourse*. Sexual intercourse occurs when the husband puts his erect penis into his wife's vagina. Sexual intercourse results in a nice feeling known as sexual climax or *orgasm*. These moments of sexual closeness celebrate an emotional and spiritual bond that can draw a husband and wife closer to each other and closer to God.

∿∿

Questions about Sex

What is *making love?* That is another term for sexual intercourse or having sex. It's a nice term because it focuses on the importance of love, but sadly it's a term used by many people who have decided that if they claim love for someone, marriage is not necessary prior to sexual relations. Despite what you may see on TV and in the movies, that is simply not the case.

Making love should be reserved for those who have made marriage covenants.

How often do a husband and wife make love? That is a personal decision between the two of them. Couples may find that frequency changes at different stages of their lives.

Where does sex take place? Usually in bed, but it can happen in other places too.

Does the wife get pregnant every time? No. The wife can only become pregnant a few days each month. The days she can become pregnant depend on her menstrual cycle.

Can you get diseases from sex? Yes, some diseases are sexually transmitted. You have probably heard about the most dangerous one, AIDS. However, when husbands and wives make love only with each other and no one else, they are well protected from these diseases.

What is a *virgin*? Before someone has sexual intercourse he or she is called a virgin. You may hear of young people getting teased because they are virgins. You may hear jokes about virginity or see something in a movie that makes it seem like it is bad or old-fashioned to be a virgin. That's not true. Being a virgin before you are married is wonderful and good, and it meets our Heavenly Father's expectation. The world would have you believe that nobody past a certain age is still a virgin. That's nonsense. A lot of people—both inside and outside the Church—choose to follow God and be virgins until they get married. It is Heavenly Father's desire that both men and women remain virgins until they are married (1 Thessalonians 4:3).

~~~

"That's Gross!"

When young people first hear about sexual intercourse, they often think it is weird or disgusting. That's usually because they do not yet know the strong feelings husbands and wives have for each other. Eating food would sound pretty weird too if you heard about it without knowing what it was like.

Another reason some young people think sex is gross or dirty is because sex organs are closely associated with going to the bathroom. Having sexual intercourse and going to the bathroom are very different from each other.

A third reason is that "dirty" jokes are so common in our society. People who tell jokes about sex make light of a sacred God-given experience, turning something sacred into something dirty.

Sexual feelings are good. God has given them to us and made them strong and constant for a good reason. My wife and I have four wonderful children who bring us great joy. We have those children because sex fulfilled one of its purposes. What a thrill for parents to be partners with each other and with God in creating a physical body!

I have a fantastic wife. She served her mission in Guatemala. She is a nurse. I call her my RMRN (returned-missionary registered nurse). She is my best friend in the world. One of the reasons we share such a happy and close relationship is because we share special moments together that are not shared with anyone else. By helping to bond us together, sex fulfills another one of its purposes.

But as with any good thing, sex can be misused. We can use a hammer to build a wall or to tear one down. Whether the hammer is put to good use or bad use depends on how, when, why, and where we use it.

If we use our powers to create life outside the bonds of marriage, we are using a good tool in a way that can tear down and destroy. Sex outside of marriage will bring disappointment and unhappiness—not just for the individuals involved, but for their families and friends.

Chapter 7

THE LAW OF CHASTITY

Why Stay Morally Clean?

Because God wants us to be happy, he has given us commandments. One of those commandments is the law of *chastity*, which means that no one should have sexual relations before marriage and that after marriage husbands and wives should have sexual relations only with each other. We usually use the words "morally clean" to describe someone who obeys the law of chastity. Some people say it is too hard to live this commandment—that it is old-fashioned, unnecessary, or unrealistic. No matter what they say, it is still a commandment. Not only is it possible to follow this commandment, it is very important.

Terrance D. Olson said that those who obey the law of chastity find strength of character, peace of mind, and long-term happiness. They avoid having babies with someone who isn't their husband or wife. They avoid getting sexually transmitted diseases and infections and passing them to their children. They build relationships of trust, loyalty, and commitment that are essential to a successful marriage and family life. They keep their reputations clear and undamaged. Most important, they strengthen their relationship with God, show him their love, and remain worthy to enter the temple and one day return to live with him ("Truths of Moral Purity," *Ensign,* October 1998, 42–49).

Adultery and Fornication

Adultery is sexual relations between a married person and someone other than his or her spouse. It is a serious violation of God's law. *Fornication*, also a serious violation of the law of chastity, is sexual relations between unmarried people.

Adultery and fornication break baptismal and temple covenants, and Church members who commit them are subject to Church discipline. Repentance is possible, but it is a difficult and painful process.

@

Homosexuality and Prostitution

Homosexuality, or homosexual behavior, occurs when two people of the same sex choose to engage in sexual activity—in other words, men having sex with men, and women having sex with women. Male homosexuals are called gay; female homosexuals are called lesbians.

The world would try to convince us that people who engage in homosexual relations are normal and healthy—that there is nothing wrong with what they are doing. They are wrong. Homosexuality goes against God's teachings and plan. In the Pearl of Great Price we read, "Therefore shall a man . . . cleave unto his wife, and they shall be one flesh" (Abraham 5:18). The Bible says, "Neither is the man without the woman, neither the woman without the man, in the Lord" (1 Corinthians 11:11).

Prostitution occurs when a man, woman, boy, or girl does sexual things with another person in exchange for money. Prostitution and homosexuality are serious sins. As with adultery and fornication, members of the Church who become involved with such activities break covenants and are subject to Church discipline. Forgiveness is possible, but sinners must sincerely repent and seek the blessings of Christ's atonement in their lives. They must work closely with their bishops in this process.

ה

Temptations and Pressure

Consider the sacred nature of our powers to create children. Think of how the righteous use of these powers can bring us to God as he allows us to have strong marriages and families of our own. No wonder Satan will do anything to degrade sex and tempt us to use it in a negative way. Satan would have us use the power that can bring us unbelievable joy in selfish ways that will eventually bring us misery instead. Satan would have us trade our enduring happiness for temporary thrills. Do not be fooled.

Sometimes people will try to pressure you into doing sexual things. Perhaps someone will say, "If you really loved me, you would do it" or "You owe it to me." Don't let anyone feed you such untrue lines. People who really respect or love you would never say such things.

Some people will say, "Everybody does it." That's a lie. Everybody does *not* do it and even if they did, it still wouldn't make it right. Elder Neal A. Maxwell has said, "Crowds cannot make right what God has declared to be wrong" ("Answer Me," *Ensign,* November 1988, 33). You never stand alone when you stand with God and his prophets. Crowds had a great time laughing and pointing at Noah, but in the end it wasn't Noah who missed the boat.

Chapter 8

CONTROLLING
UNWORTHY THOUGHTS

Some Thoughts on Thoughts

Perhaps we would never dream of breaking the law of chastity, but at one time or another we have all felt a little hypocritical because the thoughts found in our heads are not found in the family home evening manual. We feel embarrassed, weak, unworthy, and even a little dirty because of such thoughts.

In the *New Era* we read, "You are not morally sick just because bad thoughts sometimes come into your mind. Thoughts are powerful, and all of us at times have trouble dealing with them" ("Q&A," May 1989, 17). Inappropriate thoughts are a natural part of being human and a very normal part of growing up, but each of us needs to learn how to control them.

❦

Uninvited Guests

Not many people I know wake up in the morning and say, "My, I wonder what dirty thoughts I'll have today." The thoughts just come without being invited, and that is part of the problem. Our challenge is to prevent those thoughts from turning into *lust*, which means wanting someone in a sexual way.

We see an attractive person of the opposite sex and bells ring inside our heads. We see shorts that are too short, and the bells ring again. We hear people tell off-color jokes or twist an innocent phrase to mean something totally unintended, and the bells ring once more. Often those same jokes replay themselves over and over in our minds as if somebody had a finger on a bell button and were constantly pushing it. I have even read a few choice words here and there on the walls of public rest rooms and have walked away thinking, "Well, I've never really seen it put quite like that before!"

Unbidden thoughts and ideas seem to demand room in our heads even when we have placed a "No Vacancy" sign in clear view. They are simply a part of everyday living in this telestial world. President Ezra Taft Benson assures us, "Our accountability begins with how we handle the evil thought immediately after it is presented" ("Think On Christ," *Ensign,* March 1989, 4).

·∴·

"Are My Evil Thoughts Sins?"

The Savior warned, "Whosoever looketh on a woman to lust after her hath committed adultery with her already *in his heart*" (Matthew 5:28; emphasis added). In the Old Testament we read, "As [a man] thinketh *in his heart,* so is he" (Proverbs 23:7; emphasis added).

Truman G. Madsen writes, "Reread the oft-quoted passages about the thoughts. You will note that it is not the occurrence of ideas in the head but their lodgment in the heart that degrades. . . . The issue is not so much what thoughts occur in our minds, but how we nurture them in our desires" (*Christ and the Inner Life* [Salt Lake City: Bookcraft, 1978], 35). I like the way my friend Clark Smith puts it: "You might not be able to keep a bird from landing on your head, but you can keep him from building a nest there!"

☉

Getting Rid of Unworthy Thoughts

President Brigham Young said, "The greatest mystery a man ever learned, is to know how to control the human mind" (*Journal of Discourses*, 26 vols. [London: Latter-day Saints' Book Depot, 1854–86], 1:46). Controlling unworthy thoughts is important and possible.

We get rid of unworthy thoughts by replacing them with worthy ones. That's why some people suggest singing a hymn as a quick replacement method. We also need to eliminate from our lives any activities that feed unworthy thoughts:

- Watching inappropriate movies or TV shows
- Listening to inappropriate music
- Viewing pornography in any of its forms
- Listening to or telling dirty jokes

At the same time, we need to fill our lives with appropriate activities:

93

• Praying
• Reading scriptures and the *New Era*
• Attending Church meetings
• Being with family and with friends who help us be our best

Sometimes, despite our best efforts to avoid negative situations, we may find ourselves in places where lights are low and thoughts are even lower. When faced with such situations, we have to get away as quickly as possible. Like

Joseph of old, sometimes we just have to run away from temptation (Genesis 39:12).

/\/\/\

Do Something Active

We are all aware of the connection between our brains and our bodies. We can all name people who could not talk if their hands were tied behind them. However, we do not use this connection of thought and movement to our advantage as often as we should. Just as the mind can affect body movement, body movement can affect the mind.

You can probably remember talking with someone or speaking from the pulpit during a sacrament meeting when suddenly your mind went blank. You were right in the middle of a sentence when you could no more remember what you had just been thinking than you could quote all of 2 Nephi by heart. When your mind goes blank like that, chances are you have moved your body. A simple movement can erase a thought. When you want to clear your mind, move and do something active.

~~~

Celebrate Private Victories

When you mow the lawn or do homework, people say, "Wonderful!" When you get an award, everyone says, "Excellent!" But what happens when you control your thoughts? Do your parents say, "Sweetheart, we are so proud of you for controlling those R-rated ideas that are running around in your brain"? No way! Nor is there space on your school report card for an A+ in thought control. When you cast out an improper thought, no one really knows except you and God. So it is up to the two of you to bask in your spiritual victory.

Once I was waiting for a plane in an airport in southern California. I was just sitting there writing in my journal when suddenly a man came over, sat down right next to me, and proceeded to unfold a magazine in plain view—and it was not the *Ensign!* I buried my head in my journal. My writing started looking shaky. The sentences were going all over the page, but I just kept writing: "I will not look up. I will not even think about looking up. I will absolutely, definitely not look up."

Now I open my journal to that particular page with a lot of laughs and a great deal of personal pride. It was a victory—a private victory but nonetheless a victory. I celebrated as if my school had just won a state championship! I praised and rewarded myself. I remember the peace that Heavenly Father sent on that occasion—the peace that is promised in Mosiah 4. I felt it and I loved it! It reinforced me and encouraged me to make the same positive choice again in the future. I was better for having taken a moment to celebrate my private victory.

≈

Request a Special Blessing

If you need help controlling your thoughts, ask for a blessing from your father or other priesthood leader. Just as Christ blessed eyes to see and ears to hear, minds can be blessed to think on higher levels.

"Oh, sure," some might say, "I'm going to run up to my dad and ask him to bless me to get my mind out of the gutter." Dads and priesthood leaders understand much more than we might think they do. If you feel uncomfortable, however, you do not need to tell anyone the specific reason you are requesting a blessing. A sensitive priesthood holder will simply act as a mouthpiece. You will receive your special blessing and counsel from our all-seeing Heavenly Father, who understands completely, as does his son, Jesus Christ, who knows exactly how you feel—not in some mythical Santa-knows-if-you've-been-bad-or-good way, but rather because he has been there.

@

Think It Through to the End

If evil thoughts linger even after we have tried to cast them out, perhaps we need to try a different approach. Rather than thinking so hard about not thinking, try instead taking time to really think. And, more important, to think beyond.

If I take time to analyze each detail of an improper desire or a passionate fantasy, I must also take time to think of the painful consequences that will follow if I act out that fantasy with someone. I must picture having to look myself in the mirror with shame and regret. I must think about having to confess my unworthiness to parents and a bishop. Further, I must think thirty years down the road, of taking my children to Temple Square, and there perhaps running into the person with whom I committed sexual sin. How would I feel upon introducing my children to this person and upon being reminded of my bad choice so many years before?

Everyone loves fireworks on the Fourth of July, but few consider that on the fifth of July someone has to clean up the mess. Elder M. Russell Ballard explains, "We must govern our actions every day with our future in mind. One of Satan's clever tactics is to tempt us to concentrate on the present and ignore the future" ("Purity Precedes Power," *Ensign,* November 1990, 36).

·⟨⟩·

Keep Perspective

The Lord gives us feelings of love and attraction—strong bonds that he wants us to use as the center of a united, eternal family. "What you must do is learn to channel those feelings in the right direction, to understand them as part of the process of growing and learning, of preparing for a temple marriage, leading someday to family in a celestial realm" ("Q&A," *New Era,* May 1989, 18).

Many of the thoughts referred to as "bad" will someday, in the right place, at the right time, with the right person, be very good. Remember, passions are not meant to be eliminated from our lives forever. They are simply meant to be bridled (Alma 38:12). Appetites are not to be removed but to be regulated. Desires are not to be ruled out but to be ruled over.

Chapter 9

MASTURBATION

Learn the Facts

Masturbation is self-stimulation—the touching and rubbing of your own sex organs for pleasure. Some people call it "playing with yourself." It is something that everyone seems to know about, many like to joke about, and few want to address openly. Even among Church members, masturbation is a common problem.

Some young people find out about masturbation from hearing others talk about it. Others discover it by themselves. Either way, the First Presidency has stated, "The Lord specifically forbids certain behaviors, including . . . masturbation" *(For the Strength of Youth* [Salt Lake City: The Church of Jesus Christ of Latter-day Saints, 1990], 15).

Elder Vaughn J. Featherstone has written, "There is another sexual-related personal problem which besets many young men and some young women. . . . A few of our bishops feel that this personal problem is not too serious because 'everyone does it.' This is not true" *(A Generation of Excellence* [Salt Lake City: Bookcraft, 1975], 164).

President Spencer W. Kimball declared, "Masturbation, a rather common indiscretion, is not approved of the Lord nor of his church, regardless of what may be said by others whose 'norms' are lower. Latter-day Saints are urged to avoid this practice. Anyone fettered by this weakness should abandon the habit" *(President Kimball Speaks Out* [Salt Lake City: Deseret Book, 1981], 10).

The world views the practice of masturbation as a harmless, natural sexual outlet that is a normal part of growing up. The truth is that for young men, nocturnal emissions and the dreams that accompany them provide a natural release for the body. When the body requires such a release, it happens naturally, without stimulation. And while there is no evidence that masturbation causes impotence, pimples, or mental illness, or that it interferes with physical growth or normal development, there is evidence that this practice carries with it serious emotional and spiritual consequences.

Loss of the Spirit

The immediate consequence of any transgression is withdrawal of the Spirit. Instantly we feel alone and miss the peace, comfort, safety, perspective, strength, and joy we usually feel.

Dr. Terrance S. Drake and his wife, Marvia, write, "Masturbation treats lightly and casually that which is sacred" (*Teaching Your Child about Sex* [Salt Lake City: Deseret Book, 1983], 49). And the scriptures warn, "Trifle not with sacred things" (D&C 6:12).

Selfishness

President Kimball affirmed that "the Lord implanted the physical magnetism between the sexes for two reasons: for the propagation of the human race, and for the expression of that kind of love between man and wife that makes for true oneness" ("Guidelines to Carry Forth the Work of God in Cleanliness," *Ensign,* May 1974, 7). Masturbation fills neither purpose. It does not allow for procreation, and the only love involved is strictly self-love. Those who masturbate learn to think of sex as something they *get* rather than something they *give*—a selfish view that could have negative effects in their marriages.

⑥

A Strong Habit

The difference between being in control of yourself and being controlled by an undesirable habit is the difference between freedom and slavery. Elder Boyd K. Packer warned, "A young man . . . might fondle himself and open that release valve. This you should not do, for if you do . . . you will then be tempted again and again to release it. You can quickly be subjected to a habit, one that is not worthy" (*To Young Men Only* [Salt Lake City: The Church of Jesus Christ of Latter-day Saints, 1976], 4).

Those who masturbate are often depressed by their lack of personal control. In an attempt to deal with the depression, they seek momentary relief and escape by repeating the very behavior that caused the depression in the first place. Feelings of depression then become worse and the desire for escape more intense. All too quickly, the participant is caught in a downward cycle of behavior that is difficult to overcome.

∧✽✽∧

Feelings of Despair and Guilt

The world would have us believe that such feelings are of our own making or are imposed on us by an unreasonable standard. We know, however, that "despair cometh because of iniquity" (Moroni 10:22). Guilt is a spiritual signal. Todd Parker writes, "Guilt is to the spirit what pain is to the body. If you are playing basketball and twist an ankle, the physical pain gives you the signal, 'Stop! Don't do any more or you'll damage yourself further!' If you . . . feel guilty, the message is, 'Stop! If you continue, you'll harm yourself spiritually'" (*High Fives and High Hopes: Favorite Talks Especially for Youth* [Salt Lake City: Deseret Book, 1990], 98).

〰〰

More Serious Problems

Masturbation and the fantasies that are often associated with it can lead to other sins. President Kimball specifically warned against such things as *exhibitionism* (showing our private parts to others), petting (making out and touching someone's private parts before marriage), fornication, and homosexual practices (*President Kimball Speaks Out,* 10). Aside from such sexual problems, masturbation opens the door to dishonesty or rationalization—trying to convince ourselves that what we're doing isn't wrong after all. Because of embarrassment or fear, some Church members lie during priesthood interviews, indicating that things are all right when they are not, or insisting that the problem occurs less frequently than it really does. Masturbation can create a reluctance to pray, participate with family, or be fully involved in the Church.

≋

Lowered Self-Esteem

LDS counselor A. Lynn Scoresby writes, "Self-abuse through masturbation will result in loss of self-esteem and feelings of self-doubt" (*In the Heart of a Child* [Salt Lake City: Bookcraft, 1987], 116). Most young people know that without having to be told. One boy wrote, "I made my goal last week. Let me tell you, I felt so good about myself. However, this week I messed up. My self-esteem went down like a bullet."

@

Seek Help

If you have become involved with this unworthy habit, talk to your parents or your bishop. It can be frightening when we finally face our most personal weaknesses. Even the noble Adam and Eve were afraid after their transgression. They "went to hide themselves from the presence of the Lord God amongst the trees of the garden" (Moses 4:14). But could the trees hide them? No more effectively than silence, avoidance, and putting off confession can conceal your deeds and thoughts from your Heavenly Father.

Your bishop is the one who has been authorized to receive your confession and who can help you in your struggle. He can offer more than just friendly advice. He can provide help, counsel, and guidance, and he can assist you to develop a

positive plan of action to break bad habits, grow spiritually, and leave the past behind. He can become your ally by strengthening and encouraging you. You won't be in the battle alone.

Be Determined

Make up your mind to do something about the problem. A seventeenth-century French general named Vicomte de Turenne was known for marching bravely into battle at the head of his troops. He admitted that sometimes he was afraid but, he said, "I don't give in to the fear, but say to my body, 'Tremble, old carcass, but walk!' and my body walks" ("Ways to Boost Your Willpower," *Reader's Digest,* February 1992, 62). As you face your foe, you must show the same personal courage and determination.

Like stopping on a bicycle when you are approaching a red light at a dangerous intersection, you cannot hope to avoid problems by peddling and braking simultaneously. You must decide to stop, discontinue peddling, and, finally, apply the brake. It is up to you. No one can do it for you.

Learn from Past Mistakes

Although we do not seek, plan, or condone mistakes, they are a part of life and a part of any effort toward self-betterment. Perhaps that is why God has commanded that we partake of the sacrament so often—he knows that we need plenty of chances to start over. No one learns to walk without falling down. Growth comes as we reflect on our choices, figure out what caused us to backslide, and then redouble our efforts. A lapse does not have to become a relapse.

Satan would have you dwell on your mistakes and wallow in discouragement. Learn to examine your failures and try to determine what led up to the mistake, then set it aside, and move on. We must make the important distinction between our problems and ourselves. Failure is not an individual. It is an incident, and it is always temporary in the context of the restored gospel of Jesus Christ.

∴

Self-Control

Just as young people must learn to control their anger or fear, they must also control their sexual desires. What if a teenager had a temper tantrum at school? Imagine a friend throwing himself or herself on the floor, kicking and screaming because the teacher assigned homework. We would not dismiss such a display by saying, "Well, anger is a normal feeling. Everyone has it."

What if a friend started sobbing uncontrollably while waiting in line for a roller-coaster ride at an amusement park? We wouldn't stand around saying, "No big deal. Fear is a normal feeling."

As normal as anger and fear are, a certain level of self-control is required in dealing with those strong feelings. The same is true with sexual desire. It is a normal feeling also requiring self-control and self-discipline.

When desires are strong, the best thing to do is think, *Good! I'm normal! One day in my marriage I'll be grateful for such a strong desire and drive.* Then turn your mind to something else.

Chapter 10

PORNOGRAPHY

Do Not Settle for a Counterfeit

What is more beautiful than the human body? What is more wonderful and pure than true love between husband and wife? These sacred things have incredible eternal value. No wonder Satan tries to counterfeit them in the form of *pornography*.

Pornography refers to pictures of naked people and explicit representations of sexual activity (in writing or pictures) for the purpose of sexual arousal for commercial gain. It can take many forms, from magazines and videos to Internet sites. Counterfeit money may look real but it has no value. That is how it is with pornography. President Gordon B. Hinckley said pornography "is titillating, it is made to look attractive. But leave it alone! Get away from it! Avoid it! It is sleazy filth. It is rot that will do no good" (*Teachings of Gordon B. Hinckley* [Salt Lake City: Deseret Book, 1997], 464).

President Spencer W. Kimball stated, "Pornography pollutes the mind. The stench of obscenity and vulgarity reaches and offends the heavens. It putrifies all it touches. . . . Pornography and erotic stories and pictures are worse than polluted food. Shun them. The body has power to rid itself of sickening food. That person who entertains filthy stories or pornographic pictures and literature records them in his marvelous human computer, the brain, which can't forget this filth" (Edward L. Kimball, ed., *The Teachings of Spencer W. Kimball* [Salt Lake City: Bookcraft, 1982], 282–83).

⊚

Sex Miseducation

Perhaps one of the worst things about pornography is that there is no love in it, only lust. There is no concern for another, only for self. There is no relationship to be strengthened, only nameless bodies dehumanized as sexual objects. Victor B. Cline stated that most pornography "presents highly inaccurate, unscientific, and distorted information about human sexuality. It is, in a sense, sex miseducation marketed for financial gain" (in Daniel H. Ludlow, ed., *Encyclopedia of Mormonism*, 5 vols. [New York: Macmillan Publishing, 1992], 3:1112).

∧∨∧

Change Environments

If you find yourself curious or tempted to look at pornography, change environments. If I am trying to lose weight, I had better not be hanging around the bakery. Similarly, those trying to quit drinking are foolish to enter bars. If you are struggling with pornography, you must not allow yourself to go near certain stores, enter the homes of certain friends, rent certain videos, or listen to certain CDs. If pornography on the

Internet proves to be too much of a temptation, it may be wise to move your computer from your bedroom to a more public area like the living room. Better yet, install a filter, subscribe to an Internet service that filters out pornography, or do away with the Internet altogether.

〰

Ask for Help

In private interviews some bishops ask directly about pornography while others do not. Either way, if pornography is a problem for you, you need to seek help. Those who have courage to admit their struggle to a bishop or parent usually find a valuable friend and ally.

A commitment made to yourself can easily be broken. Commitments to God are often easily postponed. But commitments made to another person put pressure on us. It is obvious that a person who arranges to exercise with a friend usually hangs in there longer than someone who does not. When the alarm goes off in the morning, it's easy to turn it off and roll over unless you know someone is waiting for you. Research studies have shown that those who make public commitments to quit smoking have a much greater chance of succeeding than those who try to do it secretly. Patients who make written commitments to take prescribed medicine are much more likely to follow through than patients who do not. If you struggle with pornography and know you will be seeing a bishop on Sunday morning, you may think twice about what you do on Saturday night.

However, as helpful as a spoken commitment to your bishop can be, that is far from being the only reason to see your bishop. As the father of the ward, he is authorized to receive revelation on your behalf. He can give you priesthood blessings and inspired counsel. He can help you formulate a positive plan of action and use priesthood keys to assist you in your quest to repent, draw closer to the Savior, and claim the wonderful blessings of Jesus Christ's atonement. Your parents can play a similar positive role if you feel comfortable asking them for help. You will be amazed at the changes you can make when you stop relying on willpower alone and start relying on God's power.

Chapter 11

SEXUAL HARASSMENT

What Is Sexual Harassment?

Sexual harassment means touching in sexual places or teasing about sexual things. To avoid sexual harassment means:

• No touching, pinching, or hitting another person's body anywhere that would be covered by a swimming suit.

• No joking about sex or calling people sexually oriented names.

• No teasing girls because of the size of their breasts or boys because of the size of their penises.

• No teasing about whether pubic hair is growing.

• No teasing about whether boys are circumcised.

• No teasing about whether girls are wearing bras, and no flipping bra straps.

• No displaying of your private parts to others.

• No displaying of pornography in any form to others.

≋

No Kidding

That is a pretty long list of "don'ts." But here is one more: Don't think that you can do any of those things as a joke. As you read over that list you may have recognized something you or your friends have done. You may have thought it was not that big a deal because you were just kidding around. In reality, sexual harassment is no laughing matter.

One boy in seventh grade thought he was being really clever when he pulled down his gym shorts and showed his rear end to some female teachers and students. Some call that "mooning," and whenever people talk about it or see it in the movies everyone laughs. This time the offended teachers and students did not laugh. They reported the boy for sexual harassment. Not only did the boy get in trouble at school, but he and his parents faced legal consequences as well.

A girl in middle school thought she was being really cute when she hit a boy between the legs during a rehearsal for a choral concert. She did not think of her stunt as anything more than a joke. After all, don't people laugh when they see stuff like that on TV? In real life the boy didn't laugh. No one laughed. Not only was the boy hurt badly enough to require medical attention, but the girl and her parents also faced legal consequences.

In a high school a boy was called "queer," "faggot," and "homo" by classmates who spit on him and pushed him down in the halls. A few boys even urinated on the young man because he claimed to be a homosexual. According to the newspapers, everyone—including adults— thought the whole situation was not that serious. They brushed it off as a typical case of "boys will be boys." The laughing stopped when the boy sued and a jury decided that those responsible for the sexual harassment had to pay big bucks in damages.

Problems stemming from sexual harassment are something that young people must not brush aside. However, fear of being sued is not the only reason to refrain from sexual harassment. It is just wrong!

@

Stand as a Witness of God

Young Latter-day Saints make promises at baptism that they will "stand as witnesses of God at all times and in all things, and in all places" (Mosiah 18:9). Flipping bra straps, telling crude jokes, and forcing people to look at pornographic pictures are not the sorts of things witnesses of God should be doing.

Others judge the whole Church by our actions. When people we know think of Mormons, they do not think of just Joseph Smith or current Church leaders. For good or bad, they also think of you and me. Taking Christ's name upon us means that we must try to be like him all the time and not just on Sunday.

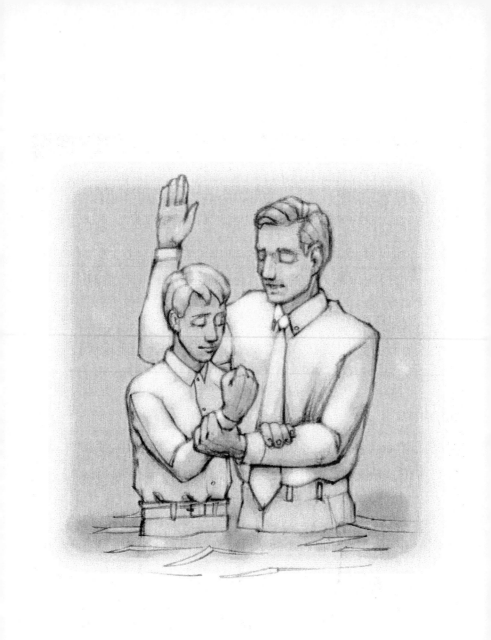

Chapter 12

SEXUAL ABUSE
AND MOLESTATION

Damage and Devastation

The word *abuse* is loaded with strong feelings—fear, hurt, and pain. Physical abuse means beating, hitting, or hurting someone. Emotional abuse means tormenting, putting down, or ridiculing someone. Another form of abuse is sexual. Like physical and emotional abuse, sexual abuse can be damaging and devastating.

·⌒·

Rape

One form of sexual abuse is called rape. It involves forcing someone to have sex. It usually happens to girls when a man makes them do sexual things they do not want to do.

⌒

Molestation

Another form of sexual abuse is *molestation*. This occurs when an adult or teenager tries to become sexually involved with someone—often someone younger. If a person tries to touch your sex organs or tells you to touch his or her sex organs, it is molestation. If that person tries to kiss you in a grown-up way or make you watch pornography or show you his or her private parts, it is molestation.

A molester could be a man or a woman, a stranger, or even someone you know well like a baby-sitter. A molester could even be a family member.

∴

Private Parts Are Private

If anyone ever tries to touch your penis, vagina, or breasts, remember that private parts are private. Say, "No way! Stop it! Knock it off!" If someone says, "Don't yell," you should yell and get away as quickly as possible. Then, just as soon as you can, tell a trusted adult—a parent, bishop, doctor, or teacher—exactly what happened.

A molester may say, "This is fun" or "It will feel great" or "I'm really helping you" or "I'm training you how to act when you are an adult." No matter what the person says, you say, "No!" Then go and tell.

A molester will try to convince you that whatever happened was somehow your fault (because of what you wore, did, or said) and that you should keep it a secret. If someone says, "Don't tell," you should tell. The molester may threaten to hurt or punish you or someone in your family if you tell. Do not be confused. Do not pretend it didn't happen. As difficult as it is to tell, it is always worse not to tell. Whether it happened recently or a long time ago, tell a trusted adult.

⑥

What Is Not Molestation?

After reading some of the above paragraphs it is natural to feel scared and worried. Let me clarify a few things: When Grandpa or Grandma kiss you on the cheek, that is not molestation. That is a normal way people express affection. When a teacher gives you a hug on your way out the door, that is not molestation. That is a normal and healthy way people express acceptance and approval. When the coach slaps you on the back after a good basketball game, that is not molestation. When the doctor touches you in private places during a physical examination, that is not molestation. When children "play doctor" and are curious about each other's bodies, that is not molestation. Early sexual exploration is common, but it should not be condoned.

∧⋀∧

It's Not Your Fault

If you have been molested, it was not your fault. Kids think, *I must just look like that kind of person* or *I shouldn't have been in that place at that time.* Even if you later feel that you might have been able to prevent it, you should not feel guilty. It is the molester's fault.

For some young people molestation is a scary, terrifying, and disturbing experience. However, other young people feel guilty because their experience was not "horrible." Perhaps they were curious about what was happening or it felt good to be touched in private places. Some young people feel guilty because they think they did not say "no" loudly enough or leave fast enough. Some boys feel guilty because they were interested in looking at the "sexy" pictures they were shown.

Remember, within marriage sexual experiences are supposed to feel good. But imitating those experiences outside of marriage is wrong. Our bodies will respond whether they are touched by a spouse, friend, or stranger. You should not feel guilty for having a normal, healthy body that responds when it is touched. A molester, however, should feel guilty for taking advantage of you for his or her selfish purposes. The fault and responsibility always lie with the molester.

CONCLUSION

A Final Word with Young People

Throughout this book I have tried to provide some straight answers to some of life's most embarrassing questions. As more questions arise, be sure to talk to your mom and dad. The fact that they do not talk about this all the time does not mean they don't know what's going on. It does not mean they have "unresolved hang-ups" or "fears about sex" as some would have you believe. It is probably just because they have such a great respect and reverence for this sacred subject.

Remember that our bodies are capable of having children long before we are ready for that responsibility. Similarly, our bodies are capable of sexual relationships long before we are married and ready to take that step in our lives. But lasting happiness and joy will come only to those who keep appetites, desires, and passions within God's bounds. As you become more mature in all areas of your life, you will gain a clearer picture of what you want *most*, and that's usually different from what you may want now.

Growing up is an exciting time and a marvelous adventure. I hope you will feel the love and support of lots of people who are pulling for you—parents and prophets, bishops and youth leaders, teachers and friends. I hope you will feel my personal support too. You are loved on all sides.

Most of all, I hope you will feel God's love, for Heavenly Father truly knows who you are and cares about what you are going through. He will be with you every step of the way. I pray that "growing up" will mean that you're growing closer to him and to his son, Jesus Christ.